Copyright © 2025

DEDICATION

To my mother, Diedra Thibodeaux —
for your strength, sacrifice, and belief in me before the world saw it.

To my brother, Austin Fleury —
for being my first teammate and the definition of loyalty.

To my son, Justin M. Lee, Jr. —
you are my purpose and my legacy. Everything I build is for you.

To my mentor, Cliff Palmer —
thank you for the bag talk sessions on Sundays that never ended and the world of game. One day, the student will become the master.

To the little Justins of the world —
keep going. You got this. Don't get discouraged. Understand that nothing beats a failure but a try.

And to my customers and supporters —
I am nothing without y'all. Your belief fuels my mission. Thank you for trusting the vision.

– Dr. Justin M. Lee, Sr., MBA

The Author

Dr. Justin M. Lee, Sr. is a distinguished entrepreneur, licensed general contractor, and real estate broker with a strong academic foundation in organizational leadership and business development. As the founder and CEO of J.M. Lee Construction, he leads one of the few Black-owned design-build firms in Georgia offering comprehensive services spanning land acquisition, architectural design, construction, and profitable disposition. His firm is known for delivering high-quality commercial and residential projects, including restaurant build-outs, retail spaces, affordable housing developments, and full-scale custom homes.

Dr. Lee is also the principal broker and owner of Fleur De Lee Realty, LLC, a boutique real estate brokerage firm based in Atlanta, Georgia. He maintains an active and diversified real estate investment portfolio, which includes single-family residences, multi-family apartment complexes, and commercial real estate holdings across the southeastern United States.

He holds a Bachelor's degree from Morehouse College, an MBA in Family Enterprise and Entrepreneurship from Louisiana State University, and a Doctorate in Organizational Leadership from South College, earned in 2024. His academic focus is rooted in strategic leadership, systems thinking, and sustainable development — all of which inform his approach to business, mentorship, and community engagement.

Dr. Lee is a committed member of the professional building and real estate communities. He currently serves on the Marketing Committee for the National Association of Minority Contractors (NAMC) and is an active member of the National Association of Home Builders (NAHB). Additionally, he holds a NASCLA National General Contractor License and continues to advocate for increased representation and equity in the building trades.

In alignment with his passion for racial equity and social justice, Dr. Lee serves as a board member for Dillard University's Center for Racial Justice, where he contributes to advancing research and policy initiatives focused on dismantling systemic inequities.

As an educator and mentor, Dr. Lee leads The Property Bruhz, a structured real estate development mentorship program designed to prepare aspiring investors and builders with the knowledge, tools, and networks required to succeed in the construction and real estate industries. His program emphasizes financial literacy, project management, business credit utilization, and community-based development strategies.

Beyond his professional and academic achievements, Dr. Lee is a dedicated father, a proud member of Omega Psi Phi Fraternity, Inc., and a vocal advocate for legacy-building through education, entrepreneurship, and ownership. His work is driven by a commitment to empowering others to achieve generational wealth through strategic planning and disciplined execution.

TABLE OF CONTENTS

Chapter 1
WHY BUILDING OVER BUYING IS THE REAL FLIP

Chapter 2
THE PROFIT FORMULA: LAND, LABOR, LEVERAGE

Chapter 3
FINDING THE RIGHT LOT — DON'T BUY DIRT, BUY DATA

Chapter 4
BUILDING SMART, NOT BIG — STARTER HOMES THAT SELL

Chapter 5
FINANCING THE BUILD — BANK, PARTNER, OR PRIVATE MONEY?

Chapter 6
FLIPPING THE FINISHED BUILD — EXIT STRATEGIES THAT WORK

Chapter 7
FINAL WORD — THIS IS A BUSINESS, NOT A HOBBY

CHAPTER 1

WHY BUILDING OVER BUYING IS THE REAL FLIP

THEDEVELOPMENTDR.COM

WHY BUILDING OVER BUYING IS THE REAL FLIP

Everyone loves the idea of flipping houses. You've seen the shows. You've heard the stories. Buy an old house, slap some paint on the walls, maybe throw in some granite countertops and a subway tile backsplash, then boom — sell it for a fat check.

That dream was real once. But that wave is crowded now, and the tide has shifted.

Let me tell you something most real estate gurus won't say: flipping old houses the traditional way is getting harder, riskier, and less profitable by the year.

Margins are tighter. Rehab costs are rising. Contractors are booked. And let's not forget the biggest killer of all: surprises hiding behind those old walls. Mold, rot, cracked foundations, outdated wiring, mystery plumbing — I've seen it all, and I've paid for every one of those lessons in full.

I'm not saying house flipping is dead — not at all. I still flip homes myself. It's fun. It brings in some side money. But for me now, that's all it is — filler money.

If you want real money, predictable profit, and a scalable system, then you need to look at what most people are sleeping on: building homes instead of just flipping old ones.

A New Playbook for a New Market

You're not going to win playing yesterday's game with yesterday's strategy. Traditional flipping means you're at the mercy of the market:
- Competing with dozens of other buyers over limited inventory
- Overpaying just to get a foot in the door
- Guessing what you'll find once demo starts
- Depending on old infrastructure that might cost more to fix than replace

And here's the kicker — in many markets, new construction is selling faster and for more money than comparable rehabs. Buyers are paying premiums for move-in-ready, efficient, brand-new homes with warranties and modern layouts.
And guess what? Builders are supplying that inventory. That could be you.

WHY BUILDING OVER BUYING IS THE REAL FLIP

The Real Advantage of Building

When you build new, you control the deal.
- You choose the lot
- You decide the design
- You set the specs and budget
- You avoid the unknowns of existing structures
- You create the product the market wants, not just what you found on the MLS

You're not reacting to a house's problems — you're creating a solution from the ground up.

Let me show you the mindset shift:
Flipping is retail. Building is manufacturing.

One is reactive. The other is proactive. One is seasonal. The other is scalable.

You don't need to start with 10 houses. You can start with one build and still walk away with $40K–$70K in profit — clean, predictable, and repeatable.

My First Build vs. My First Flip
Let me break it down for you with my own story.

My first flip? It was a rehab on a property built in the 1950s. Looked simple on paper — cosmetic stuff, quick turn. Once we got in there, the plumbing was shot. The HVAC didn't pass inspection. The subfloor in the kitchen had to be completely replaced. Every surprise came with a bill. By the time I sold it, I still made a little profit — but nothing near what I expected.

Now, my first ground-up build? It took longer upfront to plan. I had to find the land, work with a builder, and stay on top of the subs. But guess what? I knew my costs before we poured the foundation. No guessing. No mold. No demo. We sold it above asking because it was brand new and move-in ready. And that profit? More than double what I made on the flip.

WHY BUILDING OVER BUYING IS THE REAL FLIP

So Why Doesn't Everyone Do It?

Because building sounds harder. It sounds more complicated. And to be real — it is at first. You're not just buying and fixing. You're managing a process from blueprint to final walk-through.

But it's not too hard. It's not unreachable.

You just need a system. You need someone who's done it before to show you how to avoid the landmines. That's where this book — and my mentorship — comes in.

You don't have to go it alone.

But if you do go, go where the money makes more sense.

This Book Won't Teach You Everything — But It Will Show You What's Possible

Let me set expectations right.

This book is not a magic bullet. It won't make you a millionaire overnight. What it will do is show you the play — how it works, what to look for, and how to avoid the biggest mistakes that eat first-time builders alive.

You'll walk away knowing:
- Why building can be safer and more profitable than flipping
- What numbers actually matter
- How to choose the right lot and design
- What it takes to fund a project the smart way
- How to exit and lock in real profit

You'll see real examples. Real numbers. Real game.

But if you want the blueprint tailored to your situation — that's mentorship.

WHY BUILDING OVER BUYING IS THE REAL FLIP

Why I Do This

I'm from New Orleans. I've been in development since I was seven years old. As a Katrina baby, I watched the city rebuild — and I learned what it means to create something from nothing. That's stuck with me.

Today, I'm not just a builder. I'm a father, a brother, and a mentor. I've built an 8-figure portfolio by staying focused, disciplined, and strategic. And now I teach others how to do the same — because this game can change your life if you play it right.

Let's get into it.
The next chapter will break down the exact formula behind profitable builds — so you stop guessing and start building with confidence.

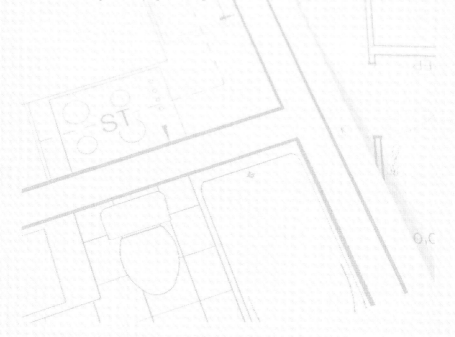

CHAPTER 2

THE PROFIT FORMULA: LAND, LABOR, LEVERAGE

THE PROFIT FORMULA: LAND, LABOR, LEVERAGE

Before you break ground, before you ever call a contractor or buy a lot, you need to know your numbers. Otherwise, you're gambling — and I've seen too many people treat this business like a dice game.

If you don't understand the profit formula, you might build a beautiful house... and still lose money.

This chapter is about one thing: **the math that makes (or breaks) your deal.**

The Simple Formula

Here's the basic layout — memorize this:

Land Cost + Build Cost = Total Cost

After-Repair (or After-Build) Value – Total Cost = Gross Profit

But real-life deals aren't simple. Each of those inputs — land, build cost, ARV — has layers.

Let's break them down with real strategy and real numbers.

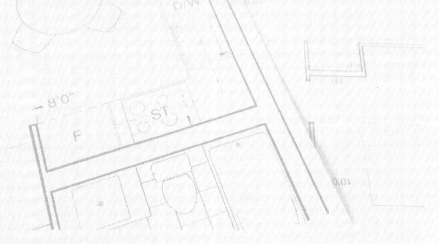

THE PROFIT FORMULA: LAND, LABOR, LEVERAGE

Step 1: Land – The Foundation of the Deal

You can't build a profitable house on overpriced dirt.

Let's say you find a lot for $60,000 in a decent area. New builds nearby are selling for $325,000. That sounds promising, right?

But if the land is sloped and needs retaining walls, if utilities aren't connected, or if zoning requires an expensive site plan — that $60K lot might actually cost you $90K before you even start building.

Pro Rule: Always account for "prep cost" — not just "purchase cost."

I teach my mentees to break land cost down like this:
- Purchase Price: What you pay for the lot
- Soft Costs: Permits, impact fees, surveys, soil tests
- Prep Work: Clearing, grading, utility connections

If you skip that math, you're guessing — and in this game, guessing kills profit.

THE PROFIT FORMULA: LAND, LABOR, LEVERAGE

Step 2: Build Cost – Control Your Budget, Control Your Profit

The biggest line item in any new construction flip is **your build cost**.

In most markets, for a clean, efficient starter home, your target should be:
- **$110 to $130 per square foot** for PEC homes (Plain, Efficient, Clean)

Let's break it down with a real example:

You plan to build a 1,800 sqft, 4-bedroom, 2.5-bath home.
You've got a builder who estimates $120/sqft.

1,800 x $120 = $216,000 build cost

That sounds clean. But let me hit you with some real-world curveballs that drive costs up:
- A foundation crew quotes $3,000 higher than expected
- Lumber prices spike mid-project
- Framing delays cause holding costs to pile up
- You get hit with a change order due to a misread blueprint

Now you're at $230,000 before you blink.
Margins shrink fast when you don't leave room for **slippage**.

THE PROFIT FORMULA: LAND, LABOR, LEVERAGE

Step 3: ARV – What's It Actually Going to Sell For?

You don't set your ARV — the market does.

Your job is to study **real comps**, not hope-based guesses.

A solid ARV comp must match:
- Within 1 mile
- Built within the last 2–3 years
- Similar square footage (+/– 10%)
- Similar bed/bath count
- Similar finish level (don't compare your PEC build to luxury customs)

Let's say your comps show similar new builds selling for **$180/sqft.**

1,800 sqft x $180 = **$324,000 ARV**

Now let's run your full equation:
- Land: $40,000
- Build: $216,000
- Soft + Holding Costs: $10,000
- **Total Cost: $266,000**
- **ARV: $324,000**
- **Estimated Gross Profit: $58,000**

Looks great — but we're not done.

THE PROFIT FORMULA: LAND, LABOR, LEVERAGE

The Hidden Costs Most Builders Forget

Many rookies run their numbers and stop at "build + land." That's only half the equation.

You still need to account for:
- **Interest on construction loans**
- **Insurance and taxes during build**
- **Realtor fees (5–6%)**
- **Staging or landscaping costs**
- **Unexpected delays**

These are "death by a thousand cuts" if you're not watching.

I tell my mentees to always:
- Leave a **10% contingency buffer** in their total budget
- Never project max ARV — always run numbers off the **low end of comps**
- Avoid builds that only pencil out with razor-thin margins

You want $40K+ clean profit minimum. Anything under that, and you're one blown HVAC install away from breaking even.

THE PROFIT FORMULA: LAND, LABOR, LEVERAGE

Cash, Credit, or Leverage?

This is where a lot of new builders get tripped up.

You don't need to be rich to build — but you do need access to capital, and you need to understand **how lenders reimburse.**

Most construction loans are **draw-based**. That means:
- You pay for work upfront (e.g. foundation poured)
- An inspector confirms it's done
- The bank reimburses you in stages

So even if you have a loan approved, **you still need upfront cash** to float costs between draws.

Example:
- Bank gives 80% of total project cost
- You still need 20% cash to close and cover initial costs
- You may need an extra $20K–$30K on hand to keep crews moving between draws

This is where partnerships, private capital, or cash reserves can save the day — or where lack of planning can stall your entire build.

THE PROFIT FORMULA: LAND, LABOR, LEVERAGE

Let's Recap with a Full Deal Walkthrough

Here's a realistic entry-level new construction flip:
- Lot Purchase: $40,000
- Soft Costs & Prep: $10,000
- Build: $216,000
- Holding Costs, Insurance, Interest: $5,000
- Realtor/Closing Costs: $15,000
- **Total Outlay: $286,000**

You sell it for $324,000.

Gross Profit: $38,000
Net (after everything): Around $30,000–$33,000

Not sexy? Maybe.

But stack two or three of these in a year, and that's six figures **without swinging a hammer.**

And once you have systems in place?
You scale.

The Formula Is Simple. Execution Is Not.

On paper, this game looks easy.
In practice, it's a minefield if you don't have guidance.

That's why I built my mentorship — not just to teach formulas, but to help people avoid the expensive lessons I had to learn the hard way.

You now understand how profitable builds are calculated.

In the next chapter, I'll show you **how to find the right lot** — the kind that sets you up for a clean win, not a slow disaster.

CHAPTER 3

FINDING THE RIGHT LOT— DON'T BUY DIRT, BUY DATA

THEDEVELOPMENTDR.COM

FINDING THE RIGHT LOT — DON'T BUY DIRT, BUY DATA

Buying land sounds simple.
People think it's as easy as: find a cheap lot, build a house, sell it for profit.

That mindset is exactly why so many people lose money before they even break ground.

The lot makes or breaks the deal.

You don't build profit into the house. You build it into the land. And if you mess this part up, no perfect floor plan, paint color, or granite countertop is going to save you.

This chapter will show you exactly how to evaluate land the right way — with strategy, not emotion.

Dirt Is Easy to Buy. But Not All Dirt Is Buildable.

Let's clear something up right now:

Just because land is cheap doesn't mean it's a good deal.

I've seen people buy $10,000 lots and still lose money — because they didn't ask the right questions:

- Can you actually build what you want on it?
- Are utilities connected?
- Does the zoning allow a single-family home?
- Is it in a floodplain?
- Will the city even approve your plan?

Most new investors buy based on price, not *value*.

A cheap lot with $50K in prep costs is more expensive than a flat, clean $40K lot ready to build tomorrow.

FINDING THE RIGHT LOT — DON'T BUY DIRT, BUY DATA

What Makes a Lot "Right"?

When you're evaluating land for a new construction flip, here's what you're looking for:

1. **Zoning + Setbacks Match Your Build Plan**
   - Can you build the size and style of home you want?
   - Are there restrictions that shrink the usable footprint?
   - What are the setbacks? (Some narrow lots don't fit a 2-car garage layout.)
2. **Utilities Are Accessible**
   - Are water, sewer, and electric already connected?
   - If not, how far away are the nearest connections?
   - Will you need a septic system? A well? That changes everything.
3. **The Area Has Real Comps for New Construction**
   - Are new builds selling in this zip code?
   - What price per square foot are they moving at?
   - Are there buyers in this area who want what you're planning to build?
4. **Topography + Condition**
   - Is the land flat or sloped?
   - Are there trees to remove or drainage issues to solve?
   - Can a crew access the lot easily for equipment and materials?
5. **Neighborhood Signals**
   - Are other homes being renovated or built nearby?
   - Are there boarded-up homes next door, or active development?
   - Would you feel confident investing your own money here?

FINDING THE RIGHT LOT — DON'T BUY DIRT, BUY DATA

Where to Find Buildable Lots (That Actually Make Money)

Most people stop at Zillow. You can't do that.

Here are the **best places to find good buildable land:**
1. **MLS**
   - Yes, it's competitive.
   - But there are gems buried in "expired," "price reduced," and "residential lots" filters.
   - Use a good agent who understands investor criteria — not just a friend who sells homes.
2. **Off-Market / Direct to Seller**
   - Use batch skip tracing to find long-term vacant landowners.
   - Drive neighborhoods and look for overgrown lots, unlisted parcels.
   - Send letters or texts offering to buy — you'll be surprised who responds.
3. **Tax Delinquent Lists**
   - Many cities publish lists of land with unpaid taxes.
   - These owners are often motivated, and the lots can be acquired cheap.
   - Do your homework — some may have title issues or major liens.
4. **Auction Sites**
   - Places like Hubzu, Auction.com, and county surplus auctions.
   - High risk, so you must verify buildability before bidding.
   - Set a cap — auctions can drive prices higher than they're worth.
5. **Builders + Wholesalers**
   - Small builders sometimes sit on land they don't want to develop.
   - Wholesalers might bring you infill lots in good zip codes.
   - Network locally — let people know you're looking for land.

FINDING THE RIGHT LOT — DON'T BUY DIRT, BUY DATA

A Real Example: Good Lot vs. Bad Lot

Scenario 1 – Smart Buy:
- $38,000 infill lot in a growing suburb
- Zoned for single-family, 0.25-acre
- Utilities at curb
- Flat, minimal tree clearing
- Comps: $175/sqft on new builds
- You build 1,600 sqft = $280,000 ARV
- All-in cost: $220,000
- Clean $50–60K profit

Scenario 2 – What Most People Do:
- $25,000 lot on auction
- Sloped, wooded
- No sewer — only septic allowed
- Power poles 400 feet away
- City permit office requires slope study and environmental review
- Utility hookup alone is $30,000
- Actual land cost = $55K+ and months of red tape\

Moral of the story? Buy **value**, not just price.

Red Flags That Should Make You Walk

If you see any of these, pump the brakes:
- Lot has been listed for 9+ months and dropped in price 3+ times
- No sold new construction comps within 1 mile
- City won't confirm zoning over the phone or in writing
- Trees + topography look "rough" — but no estimate on clearing
- Easements or access issues (you may not legally be able to build)
- Local builders refuse to bid it — they know something you don't

FINDING THE RIGHT LOT — DON'T BUY DIRT, BUY DATA

My Go-To Checklist for Every Lot I Review

I give this to my mentees. Here's what I run through before I even drive out:
- Zoning confirmed via city planning office
- Lot dimensions allow for 1,600–2,000 sqft build
- Utilities on-site or confirmed by utility providers
- Topo map or Google Earth shows lot is relatively flat
- Active new build comps within 1 mile
- Sales volume in area is strong (homes not sitting)
- No active liens or title issues
- Land clearing/prep cost quoted under $8K

If it passes 80% of this list? I go take a look.

If not? I keep it moving. There's always another deal.

You Don't Need to Be a Land Expert — But You Do Need a Process

You don't need to know everything about land to get started — but you *do* need to know how to evaluate a deal.

That's why I walk my mentees through their first few lots personally. I've seen too many people blow their entire budget before a foundation is ever poured.

In the next chapter, I'll show you how to **build the right house** — a spec home that sells fast, doesn't cost a fortune, and gives you room for real profit.

THE DEVELOPMENT DOCTOR

CHAPTER 4

BUILDING SMART, NOT BIG – STARTER HOMES THAT SELL

THEDEVELOPMENTDR.COM

BUILDING SMART, NOT BIG – STARTER HOMES THAT SELL

Alright, so let's dive into **Chapter 4: Building Smart, Not Big – Starter Homes That Sell.**

Let me start by saying this — when it comes to new construction flips, most beginners get it wrong because they try to impress buyers instead of thinking like a builder. They start picking granite, soaking tubs, and vaulted ceilings… before they've even poured the slab.

But here's the truth: **you're not building a dream home. You're building a profitable product.**

You're not here to show off. You're here to stack clean wins and exit with cash.

Alright — let's talk about what actually sells.
In most markets across the U.S., the buyers showing up — especially for affordable new construction — are either first-time homeowners, downsizers, or investors.
And what they want is simple:

- Three to four bedrooms
- Two to two and a half baths
- Somewhere between fifteen hundred and nineteen hundred square feet
- Open layout
- Neutral, durable finishes
- A yard, a driveway, and a home that feels move-in ready

That's it.

They don't want a wine fridge. They don't care about a three-head shower. They want something that's clean, functional, and priced right.

BUILDING SMART, NOT BIG – STARTER HOMES THAT SELL

Let me give you an example.

I built a 1,750 square foot, 4-bed, 2-bath home on an infill lot for around $120 a square foot. It cost me just over two hundred grand to build, not including the land.

The house had:
- LVP flooring
- White shaker cabinets
- A standard fiberglass tub
- Brushed nickel fixtures

Nothing fancy. But it was fresh, clean, and well laid out.

That house sold in one weekend — full price.

Why? Because it *fit* what the buyers in that zip code were looking for. It wasn't big. It wasn't flashy. But it was new, and priced under $325K. That's what moved it.

Let's talk about layouts.

Now here's where a lot of new builders make mistakes.

They think square footage is everything.

But a tight, well-designed 1,600 square foot layout can feel bigger than a sloppy 2,000 square foot one.

Here's what I recommend:
- An open kitchen/living/dining combo
- Split bedrooms — so the primary is on one side and the others are on the opposite side
- A pantry and laundry room, even if they're small
- At least one linen closet
- Direct access from garage to kitchen or mudroom

And keep your hallways short. Long hallways are just wasted square footage you paid to build — but can't sell.

BUILDING SMART, NOT BIG – STARTER HOMES THAT SELL

Let's talk finishes.

This is where a lot of people go wild with choices — and kill their budget.
You don't need high-end materials. You just need **cohesion and quality**.

Here's what works:
- Vinyl plank flooring throughout (no mix of carpet and tile)
- White or gray shaker cabinets
- Simple matte black or brushed nickel hardware
- One consistent paint color (I always recommend a soft white or warm gray)
- Recessed lighting in main living areas
- A clean, modern light fixture over the dining space
- Two-panel interior doors — affordable and sharp-looking

That's it.

And let me tell you something — buyers LOVE simple if it feels intentional.

Here's where you cut costs (without looking cheap):
- Skip tile showers unless comps absolutely demand it
- Use prefabricated vanities from big box stores
- Do flat ceilings — no popcorn, no trays
- Skip fireplaces unless your market expects it
- Keep exterior details simple — a clean front porch and basic landscaping go a long way

Let's not forget — you're not living here. This is an asset, not a showcase.

BUILDING SMART, NOT BIG – STARTER HOMES THAT SELL

Real Talk — Don't Let Your Ego Build the House

Too many new builders try to build a house they'd want to live in. That's not the move.

I've had students who blew $25,000 on upgrades they thought were "worth it," and then buyers didn't even care. That's money gone.

Build for *demand*, not for Instagram.

The faster the house sells, the faster your cash comes back, and the faster you roll into your next build. That's how you scale.

In the mentorship, I give people actual floor plans — plans I've used to flip starter homes over and over again.

I show them what finish packages work, how to keep the design sharp without overspending, and how to present the home for a quick close.

But even if you're not in the program yet, remember this:
Efficiency + Speed = Profit.

That's the rule.

CHAPTER 5

FINANCING THE BUILD — BANK, PARTNER, OR PRIVATE MONEY?

FINANCING THE BUILD — BANK, PARTNER, OR PRIVATE MONEY?

So at this point, you've got the vision.

You know how to run your numbers.

You understand what kind of house to build and what kind of lot to look for.

Now the big question is — **how do you pay for it?**

This is the chapter where reality meets strategy, because let me be real — financing a new construction flip isn't like getting a loan for a car or even a traditional mortgage. It's its own beast.

Let's start here: **you are financing a project**, not a finished product. And because of that, most lenders don't just hand you a pile of money upfront and say "good luck."

Nope. They fund in **draws** — which means *you* front the money to get work done in stages, and then **they reimburse you** after inspection.

Here's a simple example:
You pour your foundation. That might cost you ten to fifteen grand.
You pay your crew out of pocket.

The bank sends out an inspector to confirm it's complete.

Only then do they cut the next check — and that check only covers what was already spent.

So you've got to be liquid enough to float expenses between each draw, or you'll stall the project before the walls even go up.

FINANCING THE BUILD — BANK, PARTNER, OR PRIVATE MONEY?

Now let's talk options.

There are three main ways to fund a build:
- A construction loan from a bank
- Partnering with someone who brings the capital
- Or using private money from an investor or lender

Each one has its pros and cons — and what you choose depends on your situation.

Option One: Construction Loans

These are typically issued by local banks or credit unions — and they're designed specifically for new builds.

Here's what to expect:
- You'll need a decent credit score (usually 680 or higher)
- The bank will want a full budget and construction schedule
- You'll have to put up a down payment — often 10 to 20% of the total project cost
- Draws will be released in stages as the project progresses

Now the benefit? These loans usually come with **lower interest rates** and structured terms.

But they move slower, require more paperwork, and they're picky about who they'll fund.

FINANCING THE BUILD — BANK, PARTNER, OR PRIVATE MONEY?

Option Two: Private Money

This is faster and more flexible — but often more expensive.

Private lenders are usually individuals or small firms that fund real estate deals for a return.

Here's what they care about:
- The deal
- The exit strategy
- Your track record (if you have one)

They might charge 10 to 14% interest and a few points upfront — but they can move quickly, and they don't always need perfect credit.

Private money is great if you:
- Want to move fast
- Can't get approved by a bank
- Have a deal that can handle higher costs

You just have to make sure the project still cash flows after paying that higher debt cost.

Option Three: A Capital Partner

This one's underrated — and powerful.

Let's say you've got the hustle, the eye for deals, and the builder relationships — but not the cash.

You can find a partner who brings the money in exchange for a cut of the profit.
You structure it like this:
- You run the deal
- They fund the land and build
- You split profit 50/50, or whatever you agree on

The benefit? No loan. No interest. No monthly payments.

But — you've got to bring real value. That means you've got to know your numbers and show them why the deal is worth it.

FINANCING THE BUILD — BANK, PARTNER, OR PRIVATE MONEY?

Let's walk through a real deal breakdown:

You find a 4-bedroom, 2.5-bath, 1,800 sqft lot.
Build cost is $120/sqft = $216,000
Land is $40,000
So all-in you're at about $256,000

Comps show resale value at $180/sqft = $324,000
That's a potential $68,000 margin

Now remember — that's gross.
You've still got:
- Closing costs
- Agent fees
- Insurance
- Interest
- Holding costs

After all that, let's say you clear $50,000 in true profit.

That's solid — but only if you structure the funding right.

Here's the big takeaway:

This game rewards people who plan ahead.

Too many new investors jump into a build without fully understanding:
- How much money they'll need upfront
- How draws work
- How long it takes to get reimbursed
- What to do if there's a delay in inspection

If you're not ready, even a great deal can fall apart — not because it wasn't profitable, but because you didn't have the cash flow to survive the process.

That's why in my mentorship, I walk people through real financing plans.

I show them how to pitch to lenders, what to say to private investors, and how to present a deal that gets funded.

Because knowing how to *get the money* is just as important as knowing how to build the house.

In the next chapter, we'll talk about how to actually flip the finished build — and why the exit strategy is just as important as everything that came before it.

CHAPTER 6

FLIPPING THE FINISHED BUILD — EXIT STRATEGIES THAT WORK

THEDEVELOPMENTDR.COM

FLIPPING THE FINISHED BUILD — EXIT STRATEGIES THAT WORK

Alright — you made it through the hard part.

You found the land, you built the house, you managed the budget, and now… you're standing in front of a brand new home, ready to make your money back.

But here's the truth that most people don't tell you:
The exit is where the money is made — or lost.

You can do everything right during the build, but if you mess up the flip? You're leaving thousands on the table.

So this chapter is all about how to exit clean, smart, and fast — without panic-selling or watching your profit disappear.

Let's start with your **exit options**. You really have three:

Option One: Sell Retail
This means listing the property on the MLS with an agent and marketing it to a traditional homebuyer — probably a family looking for a new place to live.

This is where you usually get the **highest sale price**.

The downside? It can take longer, you'll pay agent fees, and you'll deal with things like inspections, appraisals, and buyer financing.

Here's what matters most with retail sales:
- Good listing photos (professional photos — don't skip this)
- Clean landscaping
- Staging or at least making the home feel inviting
- Pricing right based on active comps, not just sold ones

I've sold homes in one weekend because I staged them well and priced them right.

I've also seen builders sit on houses for 90 days because they got greedy or didn't fix punch list items before listing.

FLIPPING THE FINISHED BUILD — EXIT STRATEGIES THAT WORK

Alright — you made it through the hard part.

You found the land, you built the house, you managed the budget, and now... you're standing in front of a brand new home, ready to make your money back.

But here's the truth that most people don't tell you:
The exit is where the money is made — or lost.

You can do everything right during the build, but if you mess up the flip? You're leaving thousands on the table.

So this chapter is all about how to exit clean, smart, and fast — without panic-selling or watching your profit disappear.

Let's start with your **exit options**. You really have three:

Option One: Sell Retail

This means listing the property on the MLS with an agent and marketing it to a traditional homebuyer — probably a family looking for a new place to live.

This is where you usually get the **highest sale price**.

The downside? It can take longer, you'll pay agent fees, and you'll deal with things like inspections, appraisals, and buyer financing.

Here's what matters most with retail sales:
- Good listing photos (professional photos — don't skip this)
- Clean landscaping
- Staging or at least making the home feel inviting
- Pricing right based on active comps, not just sold ones

I've sold homes in one weekend because I staged them well and priced them right.

I've also seen builders sit on houses for 90 days because they got greedy or didn't fix punch list items before listing.

FLIPPING THE FINISHED BUILD — EXIT STRATEGIES THAT WORK

Option Two: Sell to an Investor

This means selling the finished product off-market to another investor — usually a landlord looking for turnkey rentals or someone who's rehabbing a portfolio.

It's faster. There's no appraisal or long loan process.

But you'll usually take a lower price — because the investor needs to leave equity in the deal.

Why would you do this?

Maybe your holding costs are adding up.
Maybe you're sitting on equity and want to cash out fast and start your next build.
Or maybe you just like quick flips over squeezing every dollar.

It's not wrong — it's just a strategy.

Option Three: Keep It

This one's for the long-game players.

Instead of selling, you rent it out. Or Airbnb it. Or BRRRR it — refinance, pull your money out, and hold it.

This only works if:
- The area has strong rent comps
- You're okay holding for the long term
- You're willing to manage a property (or hire someone who will)
- The refinance still leaves you with strong cash flow

In some markets, this is the *best* move — especially when rates are high or buyer demand is soft.

One of my students built a duplex, lived in one side for a year, rented out the other, and then refinanced the whole thing. He pulled out $80K and still cash-flowed $400 a month. That's how wealth gets built quietly.

FLIPPING THE FINISHED BUILD — EXIT STRATEGIES THAT WORK

So... How Do You Choose?

Ask yourself:
- Do I need cash now or cash flow later?
- What's the demand like in my market?
- What do comps tell me about DOM — days on market?
- Am I trying to build a portfolio, or build capital?

You don't need to pick one strategy forever.

You can sell your first two builds for profit, then keep the third one as a rental. It's about stacking wins *your* way.

Don't Forget the Numbers

Here's what I teach all my mentees:
Before you break ground, you should already know how you're exiting.

Don't wait until the house is done.

Run your ARV numbers, your rent comps, your investor resale math — *before* you ever start the project.

That way, you're not scrambling. You're executing.

A Real Exit Scenario

Let's go back to our earlier example:
- You build an 1,800 sqft, 4-bed, 2.5-bath home
- All-in cost is $260K
- ARV is $324K
- After closing costs, fees, and touch-ups, you net $50K

That's clean. Now let's say you get an investor offer for $310K and can close in 5 days, cash, no agents involved. Your net might be $45K — but no hassle.

That could be worth it — especially if you're rolling that $45K into your next build right away.

Final Advice: Treat the Flip Like a Business Sale

Don't get emotional. Don't chase every dollar if it puts the deal at risk.
The best builders I know get in, get out, and keep their money moving.

If your exit strategy is locked in from the start, you'll never feel stuck at the finish line.

THE DEVELOPMENT DOCTOR

CHAPTER 7

FINAL WORD — THIS IS A BUSINESS, NOT A HOBBY

THEDEVELOPMENTDR.COM

FINAL WORD — THIS IS A BUSINESS, NOT A HOBBY

Let's be real — anybody can flip a house once.

You can get lucky, hit a good deal, ride the market, and come out with a check.

But if you want to **do this over and over again**, if you want to build a portfolio, build freedom, and build something your kids can eat off — then you've got to stop treating this like a hustle...

...and start treating it like a business.

This book was never about giving you a feel-good motivational speech.

It was about showing you how this game *really works* — numbers, strategy, mistakes to avoid, and real examples. Because I've seen too many people lose time and money trying to do it on vibes and YouTube clips.

You now know:
- Why building homes from scratch can be safer, smarter, and more profitable than rehabbing old ones
- How to run real numbers, not guesswork
- How to find land that sets you up for profit — not headaches
- How to build efficiently, with clean finishes and smart layouts
- How to finance your project even if you don't have 6-figures sitting in the bank
- And how to sell or hold your property the right way

That's more game than most people get in 3-day seminars.
But let me tell you something — **information isn't enough. Execution is everything.**

FINAL WORD — THIS IS A BUSINESS, NOT A HOBBY

From New Orleans to Now

If you don't know me yet — I'm Dr. Justin M. Lee, Sr., MBA. They call me *The Development Dr.*

But before all that, I was just a kid from New Orleans, watching my city rebuild after Katrina.

That taught me something early: you don't wait for opportunity — you **build it.**

I've been in development since I was 7. I've built an 8-figure real estate portfolio, flipped homes, coached new builders, and helped people turn one deal into a full-time business.

But I'm still a father. A brother. A mentor.

I don't just want to make money — I want to help people **build freedom.**

And that's what this book was always about. Giving you enough real strategy to start building your own path — not just dreaming about it.

So What Now?

You've got two options:
1. You close this book, feel inspired, and maybe — just maybe — try to figure it out on your own.
2. Or… you let someone who's been through it walk with you.
3. You skip the expensive trial-and-error phase.
4. You avoid the landmines that kill profit.
5. And you actually build the system *right* the first time.

FINAL WORD — THIS IS A BUSINESS, NOT A HOBBY

That's what my mentorship is for.

We don't do fluff. We do strategy.

I work 1:1 with people serious about flipping new builds and building something real.

I walk you through your first deal.
I help you find the land.
I help you run the numbers, structure the funding, manage the build, and lock in the flip.

This isn't a course. It's a partnership — until you're confident doing it on your own.

If That's You?

Book a strategy call at thedevelopmentdr.com

We'll talk about where you are, where you want to go, and if we're a good fit to build together.

If you're not ready yet, that's cool too.

Save this book. Keep learning. Come back when you are.

But remember this:

**The opportunity is already out there.
You just have to build something to meet it.**

Made in the USA
Columbia, SC
02 June 2025